ISBN-13: 9780578830704
Printed in the United States of America

109 Positive Poems & Quotes To Get You Through The Day

109 Positive Poems & Quotes To Get You Through The Day

By "JUST" DALE HORTON

To my mom Brenda, thank you for always telling me that anything is possible.

To my son Dante, thank you for giving me a reason to stay positive.

1.

Morning Soon

Morning smiles
Afternoon smirks
Night grins
While darkness lurks
Fear not the darkness
Fear not the moon
Because light will return
In the morning soon.

2.

Permission Of The Mind

Take your time

Gather your thoughts

Allow yourself to be free

Always remember

You're only a prisoner

To what your mind allows you to be

3.

“Needing help is not a sign of weakness, Not knowing how to accept help is.”

4.

The Best Of Life

Take control of this day
If you never have before
Let this be the start
Of you becoming much more
There's no time like the present
So enjoy your gifts now
Don't cheat yourself of living
The best way you know how.

5.

Hurdled

Today an obstacle will present itself,
But you will be so tremendously prepared.
That you will fail to notice
It was ever even there.

6.

"Happiness is the true measure of success, just as sadness is the true measure of failure. So, keep your joy even in your missteps, and u will always be prosperous"

7.

Great Memory

You are as amazing as the stars
Shining off into the night
You are as nimble as the winds
As they blow from left to right
You are as strong as the stones
That hold the weight of the world
You are as stunning as all the precious jewelry
From flawless diamonds to pearls
You are not always on time
But you are never late
Because most of all things you are,
Remember that you are great.

8.

Formless

The damp of morning dew
Blueish the sky, sun rises
It's only the beginning
But energy flows like the day's half done
Grab it and go grab it and go

9.

"Sometimes being the bigger person,
is just being the smaller animal"

10.

Find Yourself

Destiny is a destination
How you reach it is up to you
Will you travel the road less taken?
Or follow the same path others do?
No matter how long it takes
No matter how near or far
Remember it's not the destination
But the journey that makes you who
you are.

11.

Invulnerable

Allow love to consume you

Never let hate doom you

For as you grow

Your love will show

That no weapon formed can wound you.

12.

"If ever you are to worry, let it be about necessity. Never about desire"

13.

The Color Of Life

Life has many colors

Many colors indeed

From the reds, to the blues,

From the yellows, to the greens,

Enjoy life's many colors

As much as you want, and need

That's why life has so many colors

Many colors indeed

14.

Self sustainable

Inspire yourself to be inspired
Play the role of your role model
Desire yourself to be that which you desire
Follow the you that you would want to follow
Succeed as your successor
Test yourself to be your tester
Profess you your own professor
To never be less than your lesser's

15.

*"To those who lack the will to
overcome adversity, everything
becomes an obstacle. To those who
will never give up, all obstacles
become triumphs"*

16.

Your War

Don't be afraid to use every tool
In your arsenal to win your war
Because victory is what your striving
for.

17.

What You Deserve

You do not always get what you deserve
Or deserve what you get
But it is up to you to push forward regardless of this.

18.

"Every maze has an exit,
sometimes you must take a few
steps back to move toward it."

19.

Loads Of Love

Love is not to be given
Nor is it for the taken
But love should not be forsaken
Because love is not a prison

It should be by love we are driven
So, allow love in you to awaken
Never let your faith in love be shaken
Love has always been part of living

Love is to be earned
So do your best to make it so
Its not a lesson to be learned

Yet dont be concerned
Because love you will know
If you steer with love at every turn

20.

"Sometimes you can win by walking away."

21.

Growth Of prosperity

Lush fields of opportunity
Ripe fruit of success
Fresh seeds of the future
Are all waiting for you ahead

22.

Currency Of Happiness

Someone needs your smile
It is your benefaction to the world
Do not keep it to yourself
Someone needs your smile

Someone needs your smile
Let your joy be unfurled
It is your true inherent wealth
Someone needs your smile.

23.

“Sagacity cannot be taught

It must be achieved”

24.
Palette

A dab of green
A splash of yellow
Color,
A glob of blue
A dot of red
Color,
A smidge of purple
A bit of orange
Color.

25.

Positive Road

Negative,

Not an emotion

Not really a feeling

And not quite a state of mind

Don't let negative leap into your head

Don't let negative waste your time

Negative lives across from positive

But a good neighbor he is not

As he tries to creep across that street

Allow positive to make him stop

Negative.

26.

“Pain is part of growing and growing
is part of progress,
so, if your experiencing pain in your
process check for growth in life.”

27.

Dream Big, Be Grand

Allow yourself to win
Don't stifle your success
Dream big, be grand
Put fear of failure and doubt To rest
Take action, don't waste time
Stay focus, and it will all be fine.

28.

Lax

As pure as a child's dream
As caring as a mother's embrace
As warm as a summer's eve
As steady as a rivers pace
Allow mind and heart to connect
Put all fears and woes in check
On things that happen you must reflect
But still prepare for what comes next.

29.

Never Fear

Laughter in the distance
Smiles in the near
Joy engulfs everyone
Embrace the ambient cheer
Be ready for the darkness
But don't give into fear
The light will always shine again
So, sadness is not worth a tear.

30.

"Just because a door is open does not mean you should travel through it. Sometimes if you need change you can just open a window and enjoy the fresh breeze."

31.

Power up!

Strong be your armor
Impenetrable be your heart
Precise be your goals
Know your finish before you start

Nothing can stop you
Inertia of success
One after another
Accomplishments fall to your zest

32.

Mind, Body, Heart, Soul

Calm mind

Calm body

Calm heart

Calm soul

Satisfaction through tranquility

Allow fragments to become whole

Know yourself

Know your surroundings

Know your friends

Know your foes

Calm mind

Calm body

Calm heart

Calm soul

33.

Repeat Success

Never give up

Don't give in

Be herculean

To their chagrin

You have the strength

As well as the acumen

Seize the day

Then do it all again

34.

The Grace Of Gaiety

Dream the life you want to live
Then live the life of your dreams
Everything you covet
Can be well with in your means
Laser focused
Unyielding
Relentless
And fierce
Go for what you want like a hunter for its prey
Then live in gaiety throughout
the rest of your years

35.

“Make every moment better than the last until every instance becomes the best time of your life”

36.

Stay Up

I’ve been berated

I've been scolded

I’ve been insulted

I’ve been down

I’ve been beaten

I’ve been battered

I’ve been assaulted

I’ve been down

I’ve been broken

I’ve been shattered

I’ve been torn

I’ve been down

But no matter how bad it all sounds

I rise and I thrive

Because although I have been many times,

nothing can keep me down

37.

Façade In Realtime

It may have the appearance of gold
But lack the composition
Or it may be brilliant like a diamond
But it's not even though it glistens
If it is offered to you for a price
Does not mean that you should invest
And even if it is edible
it is not an invitation to ingest
See the beauty of restraint
Is it gives vitality to patience
Allowing us to take a step back
And see the reality of what we are facing.

38.

Discovering Hope

Someone once asked me
What is hope?
The answer to which I thought I knew
But as I deliberated
To answer I hesitated
Because answer is something I just could not do
I hoped for things
I hoped for people
Heck I even held out hope
But at the moment
when asked if I knew What it was
My answer was simply "nope"
Is hope something you develop?
Is it something with you from birth?
Can you ever truly lose it?
Can hope be killed or hurt?
And then it dawned on me
That I know hope very well

Hope is what wakes me up every day
Hope is what picked me up when I fell
Hope is the future in the present
Hope is the goodness in one's soul
Hope is the voice that tells you it will be ok
Hope is what keeps us from growing old
So I now can answer without a doubt
Because I know now my thoughts are true
Hope is not just something that you have
It's the guiding force that leads you down the path of everything you ever wish to do

39.

“The worse the downs the greater the ups, turn your tragedy to triumph.”

40.

Good Eats

Nothing like a good meal
Every herb, every spice
All working together
To bring my life delight
Bring crunchy
Bring chewy
Bring salty
Bring sweet
Bring bread
Bring veggies
Bring fruits
Bring meat
Nothing like a good meal
Every chunk, every slice
All working together
To start and end my day off just right.

41.

Spear & Shield

Simplicity is the tip
Of the spear of understanding
Lead with it always
To stop life from being too demanding
Complication is a shield
It stops others from getting in
So, if you crave reciprocity
Keep the confusion to a minimum.

42.

Rule Of AU

Do you know the golden rule?

Do onto others as you would like Done onto you.

Treat those around as you would
Like to be treated

Need others as you wouldn't mind being needed

Don't expect more than you are willing to give

And live your life in the manner you
would want others to live.

43.

"An idea is only as good as the execution, some of the brightest minds fade away with the best thoughts. While mediocre concepts with great execution continue to thrive."

44.

Of Earth

You are of this earth
You share in its grace
Bask in its sunlight
Run free in its space
Drink from its waters
Eat from its land
Swim in its oceans
Burrow in its sands
Stay in touch with nature
It will always be around
It is a market that never closes
A house that you can never knock down
You are of this earth
Share in its grace
And take solace in the fact
That you are in a wondrous place

45.

Falsity's Truth

Do not wallow in falsity
Only act on what is true
Facts will cause you to proceed accordingly
While rumors can have you look a fool

46.

“Wealth starts in the mind. Be wealthy in thought first, and the rest will follow.”

47.

Inner Growth

True happiness starts from the inside,

True sadness begins there too

So everyday reflect on life

And monitor what is growing inside of you

48.

“Believe, achieve, persevere and be humble.”

49.

Point Of No Return

Grown up

What is a grown up?

Does your age make you a grown up?

Simply spending time on the planet?

Is it a feeling?

Can you just wake up and say

I'm tired of being young I can
No longer stand it?

Is it maturity?

Can you say

"Hey I make grown up decisions
Therefore I am"?

Is it something someone else Has
to bestow upon you?

The title of woman or man?

How about a look?

You look like your grown up

so, you must be right?

What about a decision?

"you know what, I'm going to be
a grown up tonight!"

I'm not sure what it is,

or how we should determine it at that

But I do know however you become a grown up

there is no going back.

Take charge.

50.

"Every part of you is great, and you are the sum of your parts."

51.

unico nel suo genere

99+ percent of people fail

99+ percent of people won't make it

99+ percent of people cant

99+ percent of people don’t ace it

99+ percent of people fall flat

99+ percent of people get defeated

99+ percent of people lose bad

99+ percent of people will not beat it

If the odds have you at a disadvantaged

And achieving seems unbelievable

Just remember that you are you

And that sets you apart from 99+ percent of all people.

52.

"Indifference is not a positive state."

53.

The Interdependence Of The Soldier And The Nurse

The soldier has to be able to kill

The nurse to keep people alive

The soldier needs to be harsh

The nurse needs to be kind

Without the soldier the nurse may die

And same is true for the soldier without the nurse

So it's imperative that they collaborate

In order for the system to work.

So whether you are the soldier or the nurse

Please keep this in mind

That everyone is important

especially in these trying times.

54.

"Seeking to prove yhprum's law while debunking murphy's, is an important part of success."

55.

Courageous Caterpillars Make Brave Butterflies

If a caterpillar was afraid of change
We would never get the butterfly
The same holds true for what we do
So welcome the change in you to thrive
Look back and reflect
But never look back in regret
Stick to the things you choose
Learn to live and expect
Everything you accept
and everything you do
is a forward step
to make you a better you.

56.

"The path to success is rarely a circle."

57.

New Sky

Away dark cloud away
In the abyss is where you stay
You may not linger around
And try to bring me down
Because i will triumph today

Away dark cloud away
In the furthest regions you lay
Do not try to creep out
Or bring upon me doubt
My positivity will keep you at bay.

58.

"When one door closes another is opened and if not look for a window."

59.

Self-Impediment

Beware of procrastination
The destroyer of ambition
Demolisher of progress
Antithesis of decision
Beware of procrastination
Companion of defeat
Best Friend of failure
Accomplice of incomplete
Beware of procrastination
Take back your time today
Don't hesitate
And life will remunerate
For your wise lack of delay.

60.

“Burgeon”

61.

What's in Store

What the world has in store for me

Greatness

Success

What the world has in store for me

Triumph

The best

What the world has in store for me

Prosperity

Delight

What the world has in store for me

A future

That's bright

62.

"When those you care about succeed so, do you. Find joy in their happiness as you do your own."

63.

First Move

A town is started by a single home

A fleet, by a single jet

Your first foot forward may be a motion alone

But it's a journey after many steps

The power of growth should
never be underestimated

But growth is measured from the
first attempt to make it.

64.

“Young fools become old idiots, teach and learn at every point to stop the cycle.”

65.

The Doctrine Of Miniature Things

Governments can be toppled by words

Wars can end by the pen

A drop of water can disable the best tech

While Microscopic organisms take
down the strongest of men.

I say this to say

That no matter how small the size

Nothing is insignificant

When properly applied

So never downplay your efforts

No matter how minute they may seem

Because your small bit of drive

May halt the most powerful of things

66.

"Sometimes behind a LOL is a I need your help. Checking on a friend is the foundation of friendship."

67.

Positively Optimistic

Tame your thoughts

Release your fears

Align your goals

Neglect your tears

Question your sadness

Utilize your hope

Ignore your failures

Learn to cope

Intensify your rest

Tackle your peace

Yearn for everything

that puts your mind at ease.

68.

“Opportunity knocks
Luck rings the doorbell
But Destiny kicks the door down”

69.

Cherish Mental Health

There is a place
Where no one hurts
There is a place
Where all is seen
There is a place
Where pieces turn whole
This great place
Is where I'll be
There is a place
Where all is well
There is a place
Where there is no time
There is a place
Where the silent yell
We call this place
Inside our mind.
Protect your self
Cherish mental health

70.

"Tranquility"

71.

"The person who fears success, and the person who fears failure are both held back by their fears."

72.

Winners Chant

I am a winner

I am a winner

I will succeed

I will succeed

I have a value

I have a value

That's all I need

That's all I need

73.

"They say insanity is doing the same thing over and over again and expecting a different result, but I feel the truly insane are the ones who do nothing and expect any results at all."

74.

Focused and Unwavering

Bird chirping
Sun shinning
Think about better days
If you get down by what's around
Just know the sadness is not here to stay
As time goes on let wounds heal
If things get complicated, you will deal
Stay focus on your goals
don't stray

75.

"Being misunderstood by fools is a compliment to your greatness."

76.

My Best Enemy

Anxiety my best enemy
Why do u trouble me so
You make things seem bigger than they are
You make me forget things I know
Anxiety my best enemy
Why do you build my fears
You make me not want to move
Sometimes you bring me to tears
Since anxiety is my best enemy
Then I must be up to the task
And remind myself, for my mental health
That anxiety is just pre excitement of something that will soon pass

77.

"Those who are doing nothing wrong,
need not fear the consequences of
their actions."

78.

The Peace Of The Mind

Take solace in silence

Quite your mind

Relax your body

Soak up your time

Forward your goals

Build on your thinking

Process your feelings

Let information sink in

79.

"Sometimes there are not enough seats for everyone to ride, so don't force those who would rather walk."

80.

Processing success

First you think it

Then live it

Get thrown of track

Then you pivot

Just always know

How to reach your goal

And eventually you'll get it

81.

"Inspiration starts your vehicle of prosperity, but execution drives it to your destination."

82.

Springboard

Rock bottom is not a failure
It's more of a fresh start
A springboard for greatness
To gain more than what you have not
Do not fear rock bottom
Because it is not an end
Cheer when you get to rock bottom
Because from there you can only go up again

83.

"Just because something worked one way,
does not mean it is the only way."

84.

G.O.A.L. Getter

What is a goal?

G is for going out and getting it

O is for overcoming all obstacles

A is for always advancing

L is for learning and labor

85.

“The first time you do what your told can't be done, should be last time you can't do what you imagine.”

86.

Assured Prosperity

As sure as rain is wet

As sure as the sun is bright

Be sure that you will get

All that you want in life

One person wishing you well

Is worth more than 100 not

If you don't quit you never fail

So hold on with everything you got

87.

“Don't underestimate the importance of relationships, even the ones that seem useless can hold valuable lessons.”

88.

Thee Haiku

Time will heal your wounds
The virtuous are patient
Stopping has value

89.

ShadowLight

Lights cast shadows
Lights cast shadows
Be aware of the darkness behind
Lights cast shadows
Lights cast shadows
Please keep your consequences in mind
Lights cast shadows
Lights cast shadows
This is not a reason for dismay
Because lights cast shadows
All lights cast shadows
The bigger the shadow the brighter
the shine of your rays.

90.

"Close your eyes with the energy you wish to wake up to"

91.

Bad Be Gone

Protect your aura

Project your energy

Absorb the love

Repel negativity

Distribute affection

Discard disdain

Avoid dejection

Embrace help to maintain

92.

"The ability to press on through adversity is a skill that can transform a potential failure into great success"

93.

I Am Just Fine

Alarm clock disrupts my sleep

But I am just fine

My car failed to start today

But I am just fine

Someone bumped me on the way to work

But I am just fine

My boss is being a huge jerk

But I am just fine

The lunch I packed spilled in my bag

But I am just fine

My computer is slow and starts to lag

But I am just fine.

I won't let the missteps get to me

So I am just fine

And whatever I don’t get in my favor today

I have Tomorrow to make it mine

94.

"Sometimes a good thing is just the beginning of something great.

Don't settle for winning a round, gain victory in the entire match"

95.

The Plight Of The Go Getter

Difficult is it to balance

Being humble yet confident

Going full throttle but not out pacing your peers

Motivating those who can not keep up

Forcing those to listen when they only just hear

The plight of the go getter

To make losing not an option

But in the process create the option
to lose those who do not understand
your dedication to not stopping.

Managing time for work

While working on time management

For social interaction

When every moment is focused on victory
normal life provides little satisfaction.

Trying to maintain sanity

While navigating your woes

Just remember to never let anyone make you
feel guilty for advancing towards your goals.

96.

"If your bad at making decisions don't give yourself a choice."

97.

Beside The Box

Never limit yourself
Always break the mold
Complacent Is the weak mind
Unadaptable is a mind that's old
Sharp as a butcher's cleaver
Swift as a hunted fox
Expand your mind at all times
And you will quickly find success
outside the box.

98.

"Show the same respect in your victories as you would in your defeats."

99.

"Those who want the world to be a better place use a simple formula, It goes as follows:

If you have problems seek solutions.

If you have solutions seek problems."

100.

Peace, Tranquility, and Life

Your ability to achieve tranquility
Is well within your grasp
Your ability to achieve tranquility
You must keep it in your clasp
Your ability to achieve tranquility
Is an inward strife
Your ability to achieve tranquility
Is very vital to your life
Your ability to achieve tranquility
Must never be undervalued
Without your ability to achieve tranquility
The chaos can devour you.
Be at peace.

101.

"Just because nobody is perfect does not mean you should not try to be. Someone has to be the first."

102.

Power Of

You have the power

You are the strength

You have the brains

You are the wits

Let nothing stop you

Be all that you are

Win the day

And true victory is not far

103.

"Everything you ever wanted is waiting for you to get it."

104.

The Man In The Yellow Suit

There is a man in a yellow suit

Looking to save the world

Everywhere that he goes he is out of place

No one knows his mission or recognizes his face

If the man in the yellow suit speaks to you

The only tool you can use is faith

If the man in the yellow suit tries to recruit
you to be by his side, will you take that place?

105.

"Know the worth of your time and knowledge.
Understand that sharing either is valuable."

106.

Duplexity

May my innocence be child like

With the wisdom of a sage

Be energetic for my years

But also mature for my age

Duplexity is not a curse

It is what makes me great

Although it will cause some to see me as contradictory, oxymoronic, and or possibly fake

I worry not of those around me

Who do not understand

The composition of my personality

Is what makes me who I am

107.

"If misery "loves" company then even the darkest of things can obtain happiness.

So while we may be lead to believe all good things have a bad side its actually the contrary"

108.

Just Dale's Take On Energy

"The type of energy received is of no concern to a converter. If you are capable of turning a negative into a positive, all energy can be good energy. If we all turn our backs on negative energy it will continue to exist in its current state indefinitely. If we all instead of pushing away the lost energy, embrace it and act as positive converters eventually the negative energy will cease to exist."

109.

Sunsets For Now

The sun shines for a reason
Life needs it and loves it
The weather may change each season
But the sun is always there for it
The snow might come and go
The rain stops by but never stays
But there is one thing you can count on
The sun will be back every single day.

Thank You!

I want to use this space to thank all my friends and family who supported me through the journey of creating this book and life. I truly would not be where I am if not for help and positive energy from so many people.

Finally, I would like to think YOU! The reader for taking the time to read and share in some positivity with me. I hope I was able to brighten your day in some way at some point and that it was paid forward into the world.

If you believe in God, Gods, The Universe, anything in between, or nothing at all please take care of yourself and be kind to each other.

------Dale R. Horton

[dh1]

Printed in Great Britain
by Amazon